'The Busy Woman's Path'

to

'FIND CALM - AMID CHAOS'

A

A WORKBOOK, PLANNER & JOURNAL

YOUR CALM STARTS HERE

A.N. STUART

Copyright

Contents

Page 8 and 9 How to use this workbook and planner

Section One: Pages 10 to 27 - Setting the Stage for Calm - Your vision and how to get there.

Section Two: Pages 28 to 36 - Structured Planning: Why Planning Matters.

Section Three: Pages 37 to 50 - Gratitude and Self Love

  Includes Templates for Daily, Weekly, Monthly, Yearly and Goal Tracker Planners

Section Four: Pages 51 to 59 - Calming Practices

Section Five: Pages 60 to 64 - Reflection and Growth

Section Six Pages 65 to 66 - Exercise

Pages 67 to 115 your journal section

Pages 116 to 123 Bonus Planning Templates for photocopying

About the Author - A. N. Stuart

Hi There, little did I know, when I first started journaling,

that it was to become a lifelong passion of mine. My journals are more than just books – they're a collection of memories, dreams, and moments of inspiration.

Over the years, they've helped me navigate life's ups and downs, and I've had more of those than I care to remember.

Journaling has offered me a way to reflect and create, especially during my time living in Italy. It was here my journaling really took off.

As I began stepping away from the chaos of my former life—managing a demanding career, running a nursing home, juggling family responsibilities, maintaining a home, and the endless cycle of socializing—you know the drill!

We women often wear busyness and multitasking like a badge of honor, but let's be honest—it's downright absurd. This frenetic way of living has been our norm for far too long, especially in the past couple of generations. And now, with social media pulling us in every direction, the chaos has only intensified.

Well, I say it's time to draw the line.

Enough is enough!

I have created this workbook, planner, and journal for those of you who, like me, woke up one day and shouted to the universe,

"Please, just give me peace of mind!" or "Stop this constant busyness in my life!"

I really did this—I'm not kidding! But here's the thing: I had no idea where to even start in creating a calmer, more balanced life. Back then, I would have done just about anything to get my hands on a resource like this, but books like 'The Busy Woman's Path to find calm - Amid the Chaos'

simply didn't exist.

That's why I've carefully designed this book into six sections, complete with templates you can photocopy and keep in your personal folder.

I wish you all the best on your journey toward a calmer, happier life!

Journaling continues to inspire my work today.
Now, I'm channeling that passion into creating workbooks, planners
and journals. These are designed to help others – not only to explore
their creativity, set goals, and tell their own stories, but ways to
overcome a myriad of life's difficulties.

For me journaling is more than writing;
it's a way to dream, grow, and connect with yourself.

***

Welcome to The Busy Woman's Path
to
Find Calm - Amid Chaos
A Workbook, Planner & Journal

Welcome!

I'm so glad you're here. The Busy Woman's Path to Find Calm - Amid Chaos is more than just a workbook, planner, and journal —it's a place for you to pause, breathe, and rediscover your sense of calm amid life's whirlwind.

If you're anything like me, your days are packed with responsibilities, endless to-do lists, and the constant pull to be everything to everyone. But here's the thing: You deserve a moment to focus on you. This workbook is your invitation to step off the treadmill of overwhelm and step into a space of clarity and peace.

Inside, you'll find simple exercises, thoughtful ideas, tips and practical tools to help you reclaim balance, simplify your days, and let go of what doesn't serve you. It's not about perfection or rigid routines. It's about progress, self-care, and small steps that make a big difference.

The word to hone in on here, is practical - yes, because that's the sort of person I am.

So, grab your favorite pen, a cozy spot, and let this be your time to breathe deeply, reflect fully, and find calm in the chaos.

You're not alone in this journey—I'm cheering you on every step of the way.

Let's begin!

A N Stuart

'The Busy Woman's Path to Find Calm – Amid Chaos'
journal planner & workbook is dedicated
to all the tireless, busy women who embrace
the journey of continuous learning.

Your Name: _______________________________

Your Guide to Using This Workbook

I've designed this workbook to be your personal guide on the journey. It is part workbook, part planner, and part journal. It's designed with your busy days in mind –
simple, practical, and approachable.
To get the most benefit, here are a few simple tips:

<><><>

So let's start by setting clear intentions!
Begin with the end in mind. At the start of your workbook, take a moment to reflect on what you truly want to create. This clarity will act as your guiding star, helping you stay focused and inspired.

<><><>

Use the Exercises Actively
Each section includes exercises meant to spark ideas and build a plan. Don't just read through them — take time to fill out the pages. Jot down your thoughts, dreams, and plans in as much detail as you need. This workbook is your journal and creative space, so make it your own.

<><><>

Let's Be Honest

The more honest you are about where you're at and where you want
to go, the more useful this workbook will be. It's okay if things don't
feel fully clear at first—
let yourself explore and dream, and the clarity will come over time.

<><><>

Revisit Often

This workbook isn't a one-time deal. As each day unfolds, come back
to the exercises, the reflections, and the action plans. It's a tool for
growth, so don't hesitate to use it whenever you need a refresher or a
bit of guidance.

<><><>

Stay Open to the Process

Remember, becoming clear and focused on how you want your day to
play out is a process, not a destination. Embrace the messy, the
unexpected, and the beautiful twists and turns.

<><><>

More than anything, this workbook is designed to help you stay
grounded and calm, no matter where you are on your path..
Remember this is exactly the type of workbook/journal/planner I
would've loved to have by my side and because of the amount of
social media to distract you it's hard to stay focused.
By following these steps, you'll set yourself up for success—
and create a life you will love.
Enjoy the journey,

Section 1: Setting the Stage for Calm
Understanding Chaos

It's true - life can feel like a never-ending juggling act. Between work deadlines, family obligations, social commitments, and the constant ping of notifications, it's no wonder chaos creeps in. The truth is, chaos doesn't just happen; it's the result of life's many moving parts competing for our attention all at once.

For busy women, common sources of chaos often include unrealistic expectations (hello, perfectionism!), lack of boundaries, and simply trying to do too much with too little time. Add in the emotional weight of caregiving, decision fatigue, or the pressure to "have it all," and it's easy to feel overwhelmed.

But here's the good news: chaos doesn't have to rule your life. By recognizing where it stems from - whether it's an overflowing schedule, a cluttered space, or mental overwhelm - you can start to take control. This workbook isn't about eliminating chaos completely (let's face it, life will always throw curveballs). Instead, it's about helping you manage the chaos, simplify your priorities, and create space for what truly matters.

So, take a deep breath. Understanding the chaos in your life is the first step toward transforming it into calm, one small, intentional choice at a time.

You've got this!

Here are five visualization exercises
to help envision a calmer life:

1. Your Perfect Day

Close your eyes and imagine waking up in a calm, peaceful state. Picture your ideal morning routine—no rush, just ease. Envision how you'd spend the day, from moments of joy to small accomplishments. Focus on how it feels to move through your day with grace and calm.

2. The Calm Room

Visualize a space that feels serene and comforting. It could be real (a cozy corner at home) or imagined (a beach, forest, or mountaintop). Imagine the sights, smells, and sounds that soothe you. This is your mental retreat—return here whenever you need a reset.

3. Letting Go of Stress

Picture holding a balloon for each source of stress in your life. As you name each stressor, release the balloon into the sky, watching it float away. Feel the weight lift with each release, leaving you lighter and more at ease.

4. The Calm You

Envision yourself as the calm, collected person you long to be. Picture how you walk, talk, and handle challenges. Focus on how empowering it feels to embody that version of yourself.

5. The Ripple Effect

Imagine calm radiating out from you like ripples on water. See how your calm energy affects your family, work, and environment.
Visualize a world where your sense of peace inspires others.

<><><>

Notes:

Expanded Guide: Letting Go of Stress

This visualization exercise helps you release mental clutter and let go of stress in a symbolic, freeing way. Find a quiet space where you can sit comfortably without interruptions.

Step 1: Get Comfortable

Sit or lie down in a relaxed position. Close your eyes and take three deep breaths, inhaling deeply and exhaling slowly.

Let your body relax with each exhale, releasing tension from your shoulders, neck, and jaw.

Step 2: Picture Your Balloons

In your mind, picture a bundle of colorful balloons tied to a string in your hand. Each balloon represents a stressor or worry in your life.

Take a moment to label each balloon with a specific stressor. For example, one balloon might represent deadlines at work, another an unresolved conflict, and another household responsibilities.

Step 3: Release the Balloons

One by one, imagine yourself letting go of each balloon. See it float gently upward, growing smaller as it drifts into the sky.

As you release each balloon, say (out loud or in your mind),

"I let go of this stress. It no longer holds me."

Step 4: Feel the Weight Lift

With each balloon released, notice how your body feels lighter and your breathing becomes easier. Focus on the sense of freedom and calm that comes with letting go.

Step 5: Stay in the Moment

Once all the balloons have floated away, spend a few moments basking in the peace you've created. Take a few deep breaths and remind yourself that you have the power to let go whenever you need.

This exercise can be repeated anytime stress feels overwhelming. It's a simple yet powerful reminder you don't have to carry everything alone.

Your Focused Day

To help you get clear. This is a short, quick overview

Daily Goals

Healthy Meals

How can I organise better

Joy in my day

What made me smile

What triggers my anxiety

My Intentions

Set Clear Intentions –
Begin with the end in mind. Take a
moment to reflect on what how you truly
want your day to go. This clarity will act
as your guiding star, helping you stay
focused and inspired.

1. Visualize Your Day

What does a typical day look like?

What small changes could you make?

How are you reacting to certain situations
during the day?

What am I eating and is it healthy?

NOTES:

2. Visualize Your Ideal Future

Close your eyes and imagine your creative life five years from now.
What does a typical day look like? What kind of art are you creating?
Who is your audience, and how are they interacting with your work?
Write down three long-term goals based on this vision.

1 ────────────────────────────────

2 ────────────────────────────────

3 ────────────────────────────────

Break Down the Big Dream

Choose one of your long-term goals.

Write it here:

Long-term goal: ________________________________

Now, break it into smaller, actionable steps:

____

- This year: ________________________________

- This month: ________________________________

- :This week ________________________________

3. Define what Success as a calm person will look like for you:

What does success mean to you?

Reflect on what success means to you and set
short- and long-term goals aligned with your vision

Reflection box:
Short-term goal

Reflection box:
Long-term goal

4. Reflect on Challenges and Growth

Challenge box

Think about a recent challenge, what you learned,
and how it can shape your next steps.

Reflection box:
What I learned

Reflection box:
Short-term growth goal

5. Set a Skills-Focused Goal – maybe it is how you react to certain situations:

What's one stressor you can actively address?

Identify a skill you'd like to master
and break it into actionable steps.

Timeline (e.g., "By when?")

Steps

- One:
- Two
- Three
- Four
- Notes

6. Plan for Calm Consistency

New Calm Habit

Develop a habit to stay consistent and track your progress

Frequency

Tracking method

- One:
- Two
- Three
- Four
- Notes

7. Final Reflection

Write down the first step
you'll take today!

"Remember, every small step you take matters.
You're creating something amazing—keep going!"

Frequency

Tracking method

- One:
- Two
- Three
- Four
- Notes

Date

Use the following pages for:

Daily Rituals for Serenity:

Pages for identifying and brainstorming small

daily practices.

Date

Date

Date

Date

Section Two: Structured Planning:
A Pathway to Chaotic Freedom

Why Planning Matters for Gaining a Calm Life

Planning doesn't have to be rigid or overwhelming. A few intentional steps can create space for calm in the chaos of a busy life. Here are examples to inspire:

1. Start with Small Wins

Morning Routine: Begin the day with 10 minutes of mindfulness, journaling, or stretching before diving into tasks.

Evening Reset: Spend five minutes tidying your space or writing a gratitude note to clear your mind before bed.

2. Set Priorities Daily

Use a simple "Top 3" list: Identify three tasks that must get done and let the rest wait.

Batch similar tasks together (e.g., errands or emails) to save time and reduce mental clutter.

3. Schedule "You Time"

Block out time for self-care on your calendar, even if it's just a 15-minute walk or reading session. Treat it as non-negotiable.

NOTES:

Balancing Planning with Spontaneity

4. Simplify Commitments

Practice saying "no" to obligations that don't align with your goals or values. Focus on what truly matters.

Delegate tasks or share responsibilities with family, friends, or coworkers.

5. Embrace Flexibility

Leave buffer time between tasks to account for unexpected delays.

Use a weekly check-in to adjust your plans as needed without guilt.

By structuring your days with these simple strategies, you'll create breathing room for calm, even in the middle of life's chaos.

NOTES:

Balancing Planning with Spontaneity (Cont)

While planning brings structure and calm, leaving room for spontaneity keeps life joyful and dynamic. Here's how to strike the perfect balance:

1. Build in Flex Time

Plan for the unplanned: Schedule "buffer blocks" into your day. For example, leave 15-30 minutes between meetings or errands for unexpected delays or a chance to pause.

Spontaneous moments: Dedicate one evening or weekend afternoon each week to unstructured time—do whatever feels right in the moment.

2. Prioritize but Stay Open

Flexible goals: Have a daily or weekly priority list but avoid overloading it. Allow space to say "yes" to a last-minute coffee date or an impromptu family outing.

Mindset shift: Remind yourself that plans are guidelines, not rigid rules. Adaptability is a strength, not a setback.

3. Embrace Mini-Adventures

Try something new: Leave gaps in your routine to explore a new park, try a different café, or take a spontaneous road trip.

Follow your curiosity: Give yourself permission to chase small, unexpected joys.

NOTES:

Balancing Planning with Spontaneity

4. Practice Intentional Pauses

Pause before saying no: When something unexpected arises, take a moment to evaluate. If it aligns with your values or brings joy, consider saying yes.

Reflect regularly: Use journaling to identify where rigidity is stifling spontaneity and adjust your plans accordingly.

5. Celebrate Imperfection

Let go of perfectionism: Not every plan will work out, and that's okay. Sometimes, the most beautiful moments happen when things don't go as planned.

Savor the unexpected: Treat deviations from your plan as opportunities to grow, learn, and embrace life's surprises.

By weaving spontaneity into your structured life, you'll create a fulfilling rhythm that nurtures both calm and joy.

NOTES:

Here is another visualization exercise:
Flowing with Life's Rhythm

Find a Quiet Space

Sit comfortably, close your eyes, and take deep breaths. Imagine a calm river flowing gently through a beautiful landscape.

Picture the River

Envision the river as your life. The steady current represents your plans, moving you toward your goals. Along the way, smaller streams join the river, symbolizing spontaneous opportunities.

Focus on Balance:

Picture yourself steering a small boat on this river. You have a paddle (your planning), but you allow the current (spontaneity) to guide you at times. Feel the peace of knowing you're moving forward while staying open to unexpected joys.

Anchor the Feeling:

Spend a few moments appreciating the harmony between control and flow. When ready, open your eyes, carrying this sense of balance into your day.

"Every step I take brings me closer to the peace I seek."

NOTES:

Date

Date

Date

Date

Section Three: Gratitude and Self Love:
Here are some ideas for getting started in your journal.

Reflect on Balance:

Where in your life do you feel the most balance between planning and spontaneity? Where do you feel stuck?
Imagine Freedom:

What would it feel like to let go of rigid expectations? Write about a time when spontaneity brought unexpected joy or success.
Define Priorities:

Which areas of your life need structure, and which could benefit from more flexibility?
Set Intentions:

Write a mantra for embracing both planning and spontaneity, such as
"I trust my plans while staying open to life's surprises."
Celebrate Wins:

Recall a day where balance worked beautifully—how did it feel, and what lessons can you carry forward?
The next 5 pages are your gratitude pages.

GRATITUDE JOURNAL

S   M   T   W   T   F   S

TAKE A MOMENT EACH DAY TO REFLECT ON THE THINGS YOU'RE THANKFUL FOR

TODAY I'M GRATEFUL FOR

1

2

3

THINGS THAT MADE ME SMILE TODAY

SOMETHING THAT INSPIRED ME TODAY

PEOPLE I'M GRATEFUL TO HAVE IN MY LIFE

Daily Affirmation

NOTES & FREE THOUGHTS

GRATITUDE JOURNAL

DATE

S   M   T   W   T   F   S

TAKE A MOMENT EACH DAY TO REFLECT ON THE THINGS YOU'RE THANKFUL FOR

TODAY I'M GRATEFUL FOR

1

2

3

THINGS THAT MADE ME SMILE TODAY

SOMETHING THAT INSPIRED ME TODAY

PEOPLE I'M GRATEFUL TO HAVE IN MY LIFE

Daily Affirmation

NOTES & FREE THOUGHTS

GRATITUDE JOURNAL

S M T W T F S

TAKE A MOMENT EACH DAY TO REFLECT ON THE THINGS YOU'RE THANKFUL FOR

TODAY I'M GRATEFUL FOR

1

2

3

THINGS THAT MADE ME SMILE TODAY

SOMETHING THAT INSPIRED ME TODAY

PEOPLE I'M GRATEFUL TO HAVE IN MY LIFE

Daily Affirmation

NOTES & FREE THOUGHTS

GRATITUDE JOURNAL

DATE

S M T W T F S

TAKE A MOMENT EACH DAY TO REFLECT ON THE THINGS YOU'RE THANKFUL FOR

TODAY I'M GRATEFUL FOR

1 _______________

2 _______________

3 _______________

THINGS THAT MADE ME SMILE TODAY

SOMETHING THAT INSPIRED ME TODAY

PEOPLE I'M GRATEFUL TO HAVE IN MY LIFE

Daily Affirmation

NOTES & FREE THOUGHTS

GRATITUDE JOURNAL

S M T W T F S

TAKE A MOMENT EACH DAY TO REFLECT ON THE THINGS YOU'RE THANKFUL FOR

TODAY I'M GRATEFUL FOR

1 _______________

2 _______________

3 _______________

☺ THINGS THAT MADE ME SMILE TODAY

☺ _______________

☺ _______________

SOMETHING THAT
INSPIRED ME TODAY

PEOPLE I'M GRATEFUL
TO HAVE IN MY LIFE

Daily Affirmation

NOTES & FREE THOUGHTS

How to Use These Templates
for Maximum Impact

This workbook is designed to help you transform your chaotic life to being the calm person you aspire to be. The templates are for you plan achievable steps while leaving room for spontaneity and exploration. Here's how to make the most of each section:

1. Set Your Goals: Begin with the Annual Goal Planning pages to define what you want to achieve this year. Think big but stay specific—these are your guiding stars.

2. Break It Down: Use the Daily, Weekly and Monthly Planning templates to map out the smaller steps that will keep you on track.

3. Focus on a few key actions each time to avoid overwhelm!

4. Stay Consistent: Each Daily Action page is your space to focus on what matters most today. Use it to celebrate progress and reflect on lessons learned.

5. Adapt and Reflect: Life happens, and chaotic events can be unpredictable. Use the Quarterly and Final Reflection sections to adjust your path as needed. Reflect on your growth and celebrate milestones.

6. Fuel Your Inspiration: Don't just plan—dream, doodle, and brainstorm in the creative spaces provided. These moments of free expression will keep your calmness dreams alive.

By taking it one step at a time, this workbook will help you build momentum and confidence as you turn your new vision for your life into reality.

Let's dive in!

Create a Daily Self-Care Routine

A busy woman often struggles to prioritize herself amid her hectic schedule. Establishing a consistent self-care routine can improve her overall well-being and productivity. Here's an example and step-by-step process:

Goal: Dedicate 30 minutes daily to self-care.
Steps to Achieve the Goal
Define Self-Care

Identify activities that rejuvenate and relax you. Examples: meditation, reading, yoga, journaling, or enjoying a quiet cup of tea.
Set Clear Intentions

Write down why self-care is important. Example: "Taking care of myself helps me show up better for my family and work."
Assess Your Schedule

Identify time blocks in your day. Example: Early mornings, lunch breaks, or evenings.
Start Small

Begin with 10 minutes if 30 feels overwhelming. Build consistency over time.

Create a Daily Self-Care Routine

Create a Plan:

Use a planning template to schedule your self-care time. Treat it like an important appointment.

Remove Barriers

Prepare ahead. Example: Set up your yoga mat or lay out your journal the night before.

Track Your Progress

Keep a journal to note how self-care makes you feel. Reflect on improvements in mood and energy.

Celebrate Success

Reward yourself for consistency. Example: A special treat after completing a week of self-care.

And remember: "My well-being is a priority, not an afterthought."

- Encourages you to put self-care at the forefront.
- Reach Your Calm and Serenity Goals – The monthly goal tracker is designed to help you focus on what truly matters, organize your steps, track your progress, and hold yourself accountable. Stay clear, motivated, and committed to achieving balance and success.

Daily Planner

· DATE
____

Today's pledge

· TO DO LIST

- [ ] _______________________
- [ ] _______________________
- [ ] _______________________
- [ ] _______________________
- [ ] _______________________
- [ ] _______________________
- [ ] _______________________
- [ ] _______________________
- [ ] _______________________

MEMO

· TIME TABLE

5am
6am
7am
8am
9am
10am
11am
12:00
1pm
2pm
3pm
4pm
5pm
6pm
7pm
8pm
9pm
10pm

WEEKLY PLANNER

Monday	Tuesday
Wednesday	Thursday
Friday	Saturday
Sunday	Notes:

Monthly Planner

JAN	FEB	MAR	APR	MAY	JUN
JUL	AUG	SEP	OCT	NOV	DEC

Monday	Tuesday	Wednesday	Thursday	Friday	Saturday	Sunday

notes

to do

YEAR AT A GLANCE

JANUARY	FEBRUARY	MARCH
APRIL	MAY	JUNE
JULY	AUGUST	SEPTEMBER
OCTOBER	NOVEMBER	DECEMBER

NOTES

Goal Tracker

START DATE :_______________

END DATE :_______________

GOAL

REWARD

MOTIVATION

STEPS

1.

2.

3.

4.

5.

NOTES

PROGRESS

Reflections

Section Four: Calming Practices

1. Deep Breathing Exercise: 4-7-8 Technique

- How: Inhale deeply through your nose for 4 seconds, hold your breath for 7 seconds, then exhale slowly through your mouth for 8 seconds.
- Why: Slows the heart rate and promotes relaxation.
- When: Use it before a stressful meeting or during moments of anxiety.

2. Mindful Observation

- How: Pick an object near you (a plant, coffee cup, or even your hands). Focus on its texture, color, shape, and any small details.
- Why: Grounds your mind in the present moment, reducing overwhelm.
- When: Try this practice during a hectic day to reset your focus.

3. Progressive Muscle Relaxation

- How: Starting from your toes, tense each muscle group for 5 seconds, then release. Move upward through your body.
- Why: Helps release physical tension caused by stress.
- When: Use it before bed or after a long day.

4. 5-4-3-2-1 Grounding Technique

- How: Name 5 things you can see, 4 you can touch, 3 you can hear, 2 you can smell, and 1 you can taste.
- Why: Calms the mind by anchoring you in your surroundings.
- When: Ideal for moments when you feel overwhelmed or disconnected.

5. Visualization: Calm Place Exercise

- How: Close your eyes and picture a serene location (beach, forest, or cozy room). Imagine the sounds, smells, and sensations of being there.
- Why: Eases the mind and creates a sense of safety and peace.
- When: Use it during breaks or before starting a challenging task.

These practices are easy to integrate into your day and can transform moments of chaos into opportunities for calm.

NOTES:

Date

"I release what I cannot
control and embrace peace."

Date

Date

Date

Date

Date

Date

Section Five: Reflection and Growth

Self-Assessment ideas for tracking your progress.

In the back of the book there are extra templates you can use for tracking things like creating new habits.

Also find the 'gratitude daily tracker' and create a new habit around daily gratitude and affirmation practices.

<><><>

Action Ideas for Tracking Progress

These will help you reflect on your journey, measure achievements, and keep you motivated: This is where your printed out templates will be of great benefit and will create new habits:

<><><>

Weekly Progress:

1. What were my top three accomplishments this week?

2. Did I encounter any unexpected challenges?

3. How did I handle them?

4. What task or goal did I avoid, and why?

5. Which actions brought me the most joy or satisfaction?

6. What small win can I celebrate today?

Section Five: Reflection and Growth

Monthly Progress:

1. Which goals did I achieve this month, and how did they impact my artistic growth

2. Where did I make the most significant progress?

3. Is there an area where I need more focus or support?

4. What new skills, techniques, or ideas did I explore this month?

5. Looking ahead, what's one thing I can improve in my planning or execution?

<><><>

Quarterly Progress:

1. What major milestones have I reached in the past three months?

2. How has my vision for my artistic journey evolved?

3. Are there any goals I need to adjust or revisit?

Section Five: Reflection and Growth

4. What habits have helped me stay consistent?

5. What habits need refining?

6. What motivates me to keep pushing forward in my creative work?

<><><>

Overall Project Reflection:

1. What are three things I've learned about myself through this process?

2. How has my confidence grown as I've worked toward my goals?

3. What was my biggest breakthrough moment?

4. What advice would I give myself at the start of this journey?

5. What is the next step I'm most excited about?

Date

Date

Section Six: Exercise –
I know with your busy schedule,
how could you possibly fit exercise in?

5 Ways to Fit Exercise into a Busy Life

1. Make It Bite-Sized

How: Break exercise into 10-15 minute segments. A brisk walk, a quick yoga session, or even dancing to your favorite song counts.

Why: Short bursts are easier to fit into a busy schedule and can still reduce stress and boost mood.

When: Use a coffee break or waiting time (e.g., at your child's practice) for movement.

2. Incorporate Exercise into Your Routine

How: Walk or bike to work, take the stairs, or do squats while brushing your teeth.

Why: Blending exercise with daily tasks saves time and creates consistent habits.

When: Think of activities you're already doing and add movement to them.

3. Schedule It Like an Appointment

How: Treat exercise as a non-negotiable part of your day by blocking time in your planner.

Why: Scheduling ensures exercise becomes a priority, not an afterthought.

When: Pick a time that works best—early morning, lunch breaks, or evening wind-down.

4. Find Joyful Movement

How: Choose activities you love, like Zumba, swimming, hiking, or gardening.

Why: When exercise feels like fun, it's easier to stick with.

When: Schedule a weekend hike or replace screen time with an active hobby.

5. Combine Exercise with Social Time

How: Go for a walk with a friend, join a fitness class, or play games with your kids.

Why: Mixing social connection with movement doubles the mental health benefits.

When: Use weekends or evenings for shared activities.

Why Exercise is Key for a Calm Life

Exercise isn't just about fitness; it's a proven stress-reliever. Physical activity releases endorphins (your body's natural "feel-good" chemicals) and reduces stress hormones like cortisol. It boosts energy, improves focus, and helps you sleep better—all critical for managing a chaotic life. Start small and keep it flexible, but know that moving your body is one of the best ways to care for your mind and spirit.

NOTES:

Date

Date

Date

Date

Date

Date

Date

Date

"Happy are the painters, for they shall
not be lonely. Light and colour, peace and
hope, will keep them company to the end
of the day"
Winston Churchill.

Date

Date

Date

Date

Date

Date

Date

"It is during our darkest
moments that we must focus
to see the light" Aristotle

Date

Date

Date

Date

Date

Date

Date

Date

"The greatest glory in living lies not
in never falling, but in rising every
time we fall" Nelson Mandela

Date

Date

Date

Date

Date

Date

Date

Date

"No matter how hard the past
is, you can always begin again"
Buddha

Date

Date

Date

Date

Date

Date

Date

Date

"I let go of perfection and
embrace progress."

Date

Date

Date

Date

Date

Date

Date

The templates on the following pages are for
you to photocopy and to print out as you need..
Add them to your personal folder.

Daily Planner

Today's pledge

· TO DO LIST

- [ ]
- [ ]
- [ ]
- [ ]
- [ ]
- [ ]
- [ ]
- [ ]
- [ ]

MEMO

· TIME TABLE

5am	
6am	
7am	
8am	
9am	
10am	
11am	
12:00	
1pm	
2pm	
3pm	
4pm	
5pm	
6pm	
7pm	
8pm	
9pm	
10pm	

WEEKLY PLANNER

Monday	Tuesday

Wednesday	Thursday

Friday	Saturday

Sunday	Notes:

Monthly Planner

JAN	FEB	MAR	APR	MAY	JUN
JUL	AUG	SEP	OCT	NOV	DEC

Monday	Tuesday	Wednesday	Thursday	Friday	Saturday	Sunday

notes

to do

YEAR AT A GLANCE

JANUARY

FEBRUARY

MARCH

APRIL

MAY

JUNE

JULY

AUGUST

SEPTEMBER

OCTOBER

NOVEMBER

DECEMBER

NOTES

GRATITUDE JOURNAL

DATE

S   M   T   W   T   F   S

TAKE A MOMENT EACH DAY TO REFLECT ON THE THINGS YOU'RE THANKFUL FOR

TODAY I'M GRATEFUL FOR

1

2

3

THINGS THAT MADE ME SMILE TODAY

SOMETHING THAT INSPIRED ME TODAY

PEOPLE I'M GRATEFUL TO HAVE IN MY LIFE

Daily Affirmation

NOTES & FREE THOUGHTS

Goal Tracker

START DATE : _______________

END DATE : _______________

GOAL

REWARD

MOTIVATION

STEPS

1.

2.

3.

4.

5.

NOTES

PROGRESS

Habit Tracker

WEEK OF ________________________________

H A B I T	MON	TUE	WED	THU	FRI	SAT	SUN

100 Day Challenge

Start : _______________   Name : _______________

(1) (2) (3) (4) (5) (6) (7) (8) (9) (10)

(11) (12) (13) (14) (15) (16) (17) (18) (19) (20)

(21) (22) (23) (24) (25) (26) (27) (28) (29) (30)

(31) (32) (33) (34) (35) (36) (37) (38) (39) (40)

(41) (42) (43) (44) (45) (46) (47) (48) (49) (50)

(51) (52) (53) (54) (55) (56) (57) (58) (59) (60)

(61) (62) (63) (64) (65) (66) (67) (68) (69) (70)

(71) (72) (73) (74) (75) (76) (77) (78) (79) (80)

(81) (82) (83) (84) (85) (86) (87) (88) (89) (90)

(91) (92) (93) (94) (95) (96) (97) (98) (99) (100)

So there you have it my now very calm friends.

I hope you have gained insight into your chaotic life and now it's a thing of the past.

Join me at

https://www.facebook.com/anstuartwriter/

Don't forget to leave me a review - they mean so much to me.

**Books by this author
available on Amazon:**

"Creating a Life of Art in Italy"

"Italy's Lasting Legacy"

**"The Artist's Path: Dreams To Reality - A Journal &
Workbook For All Artists".**

www.ingramcontent.com/pod-product-compliance
Lightning Source LLC
Chambersburg PA
CBHW060948050726
47592CB00003B/1158